Self-Representation and Pretrial Allegations of Ineffective Assistance of Counsel

A Comprehensive Analysis of _Faretta_ and _Nelson_ Issues in Florida

By

Angela D. McCravy

ISBN: 1-4033-6064-2 (e-book)
ISBN: 1-4033-6065-0 (Paperback)

Library of Congress Control Number: 2002093626

This book is printed on acid free paper.

Printed in the United States of America
Bloomington, IN

1stBooks - rev. 04/18/03

ACKNOWLEDGMENTS

I would like to extend my appreciation to the Honorable Susan Schaeffer of Clearwater, Florida, who gave me my first opportunity to see how much excitement there can be in legal research and writing.

Also, much thanks to Assistant State Attorney David Foxman for the generous contribution of his legal acumen and editing skills.

Gratitude is also owed to the office computer guru, Assistant Attorney General Carmen Corrente, for his invaluable assistance in making my computer do what I needed it to do when I needed it to do it.

This book is dedicated to my third grade teacher, Dorothy Brown, who taught me more than she will ever know.

"*Most people - one may say the best sort of people - greatly prefer to do things for themselves, however badly, than to have things done for them, however well.*"

Anonymous

TABLE OF CONTENTS

PREFACE xi

CHAPTER ONE: WHEN A DEFENDANT
COMPLAINS ABOUT COURT-APPOINTED
COUNSEL 1
  Defendant wants to replace court-
  appointed counsel with private
  counsel 1
  Defendant wants to replace court-
  appointed counsel with different
  court-appointed counsel 3
  The timing of the motion 3
  The sufficiency of the
  allegations 4
  The Nelson inquiry 6
  Appellate review 12

CHAPTER TWO: WHEN A DEFENDANT
REQUESTS SELF-REPRESENTATION 15
  The timing of the request 15
  The nature of the request 17
  Subsequent waiver of the right
  to self-representation 18
  The nature of the Faretta
  inquiry 19
  Dangers and disadvantages of
  self-representation 21
  Legal knowledge, skill and
  experience 23

Ability and willingness to abide by the rules of courtroom procedure and protocol 30
Renewal of the offer of assistance of counsel 32
Special Factors 34
Defendants who misbehave 34
Erroneous claims of insolvency 36
Defendants who have mental problems 37
Juveniles 38
Self-representation in collateral proceedings 41

CHAPTER THREE: STANDBY COUNSEL AND HYBRID REPRESENTATION 43

CHAPTER FOUR: THE APPEAL PROCESS .. 49
Self-representation on appeal ... 49
Appellate review of Nelson/Faretta issues 53

CONCLUSION 57

APPENDIX 61
Trial Stage Faretta Inquiry 63
Plea Stage Faretta Inquiry 72
Form 8.933 Juvenile Waiver of Counsel 77

PREFACE

The Sixth Amendment of the United States Constitution guarantees effective assistance of counsel to each individual charged with a crime. It has been said that, of all rights guaranteed to an accused person, the right to counsel is the most significant.[1] However, "[t]o thrust counsel upon a defendant, against his considered wish, violates the logic of the Sixth Amendment of the United States Constitution, which guarantees rights necessary to a full defense, including the implied right to self-representation."[2] Because of this right to decline counsel, in the absence of unusual circumstances, an accused who is mentally competent has the right to conduct his or her own defense.[3]

Allegations by a defendant that he or she is not receiving effective assistance of counsel, as well as requests for self-representation, are stressful events in today's criminal courtrooms - events which are happening with more and more frequency. A defendant may

---

[1] **United States v. Chronic**, 466 U.S. 648, 654 (1984).

[2] **Faretta v. California**, 422 U.S. 806, 820-21 (1975).

[3] **Kimble v. State**, 429 So. 2d 1369 (Fla. 3d DCA 1983).

understandably feel alarmed if he or she believes stellar representation is not being provided when liberty is at stake. As a result, the defendant may wish to exert more control over the presentation of the defense, and may believe that he or she will fare better proceeding without counsel even though lacking in legal knowledge and skill. In response, the prosecutor may be concerned about the prospect of a criminal defendant cross-examining an already traumatized victim, and about being perceived by the jury as a "bully" when making objections during trial. On the other side, defense attorneys may be unfamiliar with the exact nature of their responsibilities if appointed to act as standby counsel - one of the self-representation options discussed in Chapter Three.

In the middle of this, the trial judge is sure to be frustrated at having to protect what may be perceived as conflicting interests: the defendant's right to a fair trial and the right to self-representation. "An overprotective judge who refuses to allow a defendant to jeopardize his own defense may be reversed, [] and a judge who does not make a copious inquiry into the thought process[es] of the accused (which may themselves be characterized as trial strategy) is subject to an appeal[.]"[4]

This book is designed to assist all those affected by pretrial allegations of ineffective assistance of counsel and requests for self-representation. The goal is to clarify the responsibilities of the prosecutor, the defense attorney and the trial judge when these issues arise.

---

[4] **United States v. McDowell**, 814 F.2d 245 (6th Cir. 1987), *cert. denied*, 484 U.S. 980 (1987).

CHAPTER ONE

WHEN A DEFENDANT COMPLAINS ABOUT COURT APPOINTED COUNSEL

Defendant wants to replace court-appointed counsel with private counsel

In 1973, the Fourth District Court of Appeal announced that when a defendant requests discharge of court-appointed counsel before trial, the judge should inquire of the defendant as to the reason for the request. If incompetency of counsel is assigned as the reason, the judge should conduct an inquiry to determine whether there is cause to believe that counsel is not rendering effective assistance.[5] The purpose of this so-called "<u>Nelson</u> inquiry" is to determine whether a defendant is entitled to the appointment of different court-appointed counsel because his or her current counsel is providing sub-standard represen-tation. Therefore a <u>Nelson</u> inquiry is required only when a defendant makes allegations that *court-appointed*

---

[5] **Nelson v. State**, 274 So. 2d 256 (Fla. 4th DCA 1973), *cited with approval in* **Hardwick v. State**, 521 So. 2d 1071, 1074-75 (Fla. 1988), *cert. denied*, 488 U.S. 871 (1988).

counsel is rendering ineffective assistance and requests the appointment of a different attorney. If a defendant complains about court-appointed counsel and wants to replace him or her with *private* counsel, a <u>Nelson</u> hearing is not appropriate. In such a case the defendant should be permitted to fire court-appointed counsel and take private counsel of his or her choice.[6] An erroneous denial of the right to be represented by privately-retained counsel of choice is per se prejudicial.[7]

However, a defendant does not have the right to replace court-appointed counsel with private counsel if the request is made in bad faith, for the sake of arbitrary delay, or to otherwise subvert the judicial proceedings.[8] If a trial judge denies a request for continuance to allow the defendant time to obtain private counsel because the judge feels the motion is made for the purpose of simply delaying the trial or some other concern over the defendant's motives, the judge should clearly

---

[6] **Foster v. State**, 704 So. 2d 169 (Fla. 4th DCA 1997), *appeal after remand*, 732 So. 2d 22 (Fla. 4th DCA 1999).

[7] **Id.**

[8] **Holley v. State**, 484 So. 2d 634 (Fla. 1st DCA 1986), *rev. denied*, 492 So. 2d 1335 (Fla. 1986); **Cartwright v. State**, 565 So. 2d 784 (Fla. 5th DCA 1990); **Hurtado v. State**, 760 So. 2d 279 (Fla. 4th DCA 2000).

place those reasons on the record.[9] In denying such a request for continuance, the judge must still conduct a _Nelson_ inquiry to ensure that the defendant is proceeding to trial with effective counsel.

Defendant wants to replace court-appointed counsel with different court-appointed counsel

The timing of the motion

A trial court is required to make an inquiry of the defendant as to the reason for the request to discharge counsel "where the defendant, *before the commencement of trial*, makes it appear to the trial judge that he desires to discharge his court appointed counsel[.]"[10] [Emphasis added]. This language has been interpreted strictly by Florida courts, which have held that no _Nelson_ inquiry is required when a motion to discharge counsel is made for the first time after the trial has already begun.[11] "The rule in _Nelson_ was designed as a prophylactic measure to prevent a trial from

---

[9] **Foster**.

[10] **Nelson**, 274 So. 2d at 258-59.

[11] **Haugabook v. State**, 689 So. 2d 1245 (Fla. 4th DCA 1997), *appeal after remand*, 795 So. 2d 73 (Fla. 4th DCA 2001); **Dukes v. State**, 503 So. 2d 455 (Fla. 2d DCA 1987).

commencing--not to abort a trial already in progress."[12]

If the defendant moves to discharge his or her counsel after the verdict has been rendered but prior to sentencing, the court should still conduct a <u>Nelson</u> inquiry, as long as the allegations pertain to counsel's preparedness for the pending sentencing hearing.[13]

If a defendant has made a motion to discharge counsel which is denied by the trial court long before trial, the defendant bears the burden of renewing his motion at the time of trial. Otherwise appellate review of the denial of his motion to discharge counsel may be waived.[14]

The sufficiency of the allegations

Sometimes a defendant will voice complaints about his or her attorney that, at the root, are nothing more than a reflection of personality differences between the defendant and

---

[12] **Haugabook**. A defendant who alleges ineffective assistance of counsel during the course of the trial will have the opportunity, if necessary, to obtain post-trial relief through **Florida Rule of Criminal Procedure 3.850.**

[13] **Lockwood v. State**, 608 So. 2d 133 (Fla. 4th DCA 1992), *appeal after remand*, 632 So. 2d 293 (Fla. 4th DCA 1994); **Haugabook**.

[14] **Moore v. State**, 778 So. 2d 1054 (Fla. 4th DCA 2001).

counsel. In such a situation, an accused is not entitled to the appointment of counsel of his or her choice.[15] The Sixth Amendment does not guarantee a meaningful relationship between the accused and counsel.[16] The trial court's inquiry should focus on the adversarial process, not on the harmoniousness of the attorney-client relationship.[17]

When a defendant's dissatisfaction with counsel is articulated in terms of general complaints or a loss of confidence which do not suggest ineffectiveness, the trial court is not required to conduct any further inquiry.[18] Specifically, a defendant's complaint that court-appointed counsel believes he or she is guilty is insufficient to trigger the requirement of a full _Nelson_ inquiry.[19] Similarly, the mere allegation of a conflict of interest does not give rise to the necessity of a _Nelson_ inquiry unless the defendant advises the trial court as to the nature of the perceived

---

[15] **Wheat v. United States**, 486 U.S. 153 (1988).

[16] **Morris v. Slappy**, 461 U.S. 1 (1983).

[17] **Cronic**.

[18] **Tucker v. State**, 754 So. 2d 89 (Fla. 2d DCA 2000), _rev. denied_, 770 So. 2d 162 (Fla. 2000); **Augsberger v. State**, 655 So. 2d 1202 (Fla. 2d DCA 1995).

[19] **Tucker**.

conflict and how it may impact the quality of legal representation.[20]

Another prevalent claim made by defendants about court-appointed counsel is that the attorney has not made sufficient visits to the jail to discuss the case. If this is the extent of the defendant's complaint and he or she raises no instance of incompetency or inadequacy in the handling of the defense, the trial judge is not required to conduct a Nelson inquiry.[21]

The *Nelson* inquiry

If the defendant voices facially sufficient and timely complaints about court-appointed counsel and asks the judge to appoint different counsel, the judge must conduct a Nelson inquiry to determine whether trial counsel has in fact been ineffective. As part of this hearing, the judge should inquire of both the defendant and the attorney about the circumstances surrounding the complaint. Only after inquiring of both the defendant and counsel can the judge determine whether the omission or act occurred, and whether it constitutes a "specific, serious deficiency measurably below that of

---

[20] **Gaines v. State**, 706 So. 2d 47 (Fla. 5th DCA 1998).

[21] **Kenney v. State**, 611 So. 2d 575 (Fla. 1st DCA 1992); **Augsberger**.

professionally competent counsel[.]"[22]

It is undisputed that when
allegations of ineffectiveness are
made *post-trial*, the defendant
automatically waives any
attorney/client privilege in communications pertaining to the
allegations. As such, during a
postconviction evidentiary hearing
counsel may properly reveal
communications between himself or
herself and the defendant, even over
objection of the defendant, which
would otherwise qualify as
privileged.[23]

However when the allegations of
ineffectiveness are made *before*
trial, it is unclear whether the same
automatic waiver of the
attorney/client privilege occurs. The
Second District Court of Appeal
appears to be the only Florida
appellate court to have addressed
this issue. In <u>Jones v. State</u>, 658
So. 2d 122 (Fla. 2d DCA 1995),
receded from on other grounds, <u>Bowen
v. State</u>, 677 So. 2d 863 (Fla. 2d DCA
1996), Judge Altenbernd noted the
problem surrounding confidential
communications between attorney and
client in footnote 4 of his
concurring opinion and suggested that

---

[22] **Phillips v. State**, 608 So. 2d 778
(Fla. 1992), *cert. denied*, 509 U.S. 908
(1993).

[23] **Reed v. State**, 640 So. 2d 1094 (Fla.
1994).

during the <u>Nelson</u> inquiry, "[q]uestions may need to be carefully tailored to avoid these problems. Occasionally, an *in camera* inquiry may be useful."

However, five years later in <u>Tucker v. State</u>, 754 So. 2d 89 (Fla. 2d DCA 2000), *app. dism.*, 770 So. 2d 162 (Fla. 2000), a case in which defense counsel refused to answer questions in a pretrial <u>Nelson</u> inquiry without a waiver of the attorney/client privilege by the defendant, the Second District stated in a footnote that "Tucker's attorney may have been mistaken for being concerned about attorney-client privilege."

There appears to be no justification for applying different standards and rules for pretrial and post-trial allegations of in-effectiveness when analyzing whether a waiver of the attorney/client privilege has occurred. In either posture, the necessity for the inquiry is of the defendant's own making. Moreover, counsel's explanation for his or her actions is a critical factor in the trial court's determination of whether counsel has in fact been ineffective. As the Supreme Court explained:

The reasonableness of counsel's actions may be determined or substantially influenced by the defendant's own statements or actions. Counsel's actions are usually based, quite properly, on informed strategic choices made by the defendant and on

8

information supplied by the defendant. In particular, what investigation decisions are reasonable depends critically on such information.

For example, when the facts that support a certain potential line of defense are generally known to counsel because of what the defendant has said, the need for further investigation may be considered diminished or eliminated altogether. And when a defendant has given counsel reason to believe that pursuing certain investigations would be fruitless or even harmful, counsel's failure to pursue those investigations may not later be challenged as unreasonable. In short, inquiry into counsel's conversations with the defendant may be critical to a proper assessment of counsel's investigation decisions, just as it may be critical to a proper assessment of other litigation decisions.[24]

Since it has not clearly been established whether an automatic waiver of privilege results when pretrial allegations of ineffectiveness are made, the safest course would be for the court to attempt to obtain a waiver of the attorney/client privilege from the defendant on the record at the beginning of the Nelson inquiry. Sometimes the realization that trial strategy may need to be divulged in order to pursue the ineffectiveness claim will cause the defendant to withdraw the allegation altogether. But if the defendant declines to make the waiver and insists on pursuing

---

[24] **Strickland v. Washington**, 466 U.S. 668, 691 (1984).

the claim of ineffectiveness, then obviously a thorough <u>Nelson</u> inquiry may not be possible. The court may decline to make a finding of ineffectiveness on that basis.[25] Alternatively, based upon <u>Strickland</u>, the trial court may make a finding that the defendant has implicitly waived the attorney/client privilege. Counsel may thereafter be required to answer narrowly-tailored questions pertaining to the allegations. Of course, the court may also wish to exercise its discretion and hold an *in camera* hearing as suggested in <u>Jones</u>.

There is no easy formula for determining whether an attorney's particular act or omission constitutes ineffective assistance, and Florida courts have made this determination on a case by case basis. One common complaint is that the attorney has refused to perform exactly as the defendant has instructed. As a general rule, a defendant does not have the right to choreograph an attorney's performance.[26] Even so, the judge must inquire of both the defendant and the attorney as to exactly what the defendant wishes the attorney to do, and why the attorney has not complied with the request.

---

[25] **Tucker**.
[26] **McKaskle v. Wiggins**, 465 U.S. 168 (1994).

After the _Nelson_ inquiry, if the judge determines that court-appointed counsel has in fact been ineffective, the judge should make that finding on the record and appoint a substitute attorney. The new attorney should be allowed adequate time to prepare for trial.

Alternatively, if the judge determines that the attorney has rendered effective representation, that finding should also clearly be made on the record. The judge should then advise the defendant that if counsel is discharged, the state may not be required to appoint another one. If the defendant continues to demand the dismissal of court-appointed counsel, then it is presumed that he or she is exercising the right to self-representation.[27] The trial judge may then discharge the attorney and require the defendant to proceed without representation. But the judge must first conduct a _Faretta_ inquiry to determine if the defendant's waiver of counsel is knowing and intelligent. The proper procedure for conducting a _Faretta_ inquiry is discussed in Chapter Two.

The court may elect to advise a defendant about the right to self-representation when he or she complains about court-appointed counsel prior to the commencement of

---

[27] **Hardwick**.

trial.[28] However the court has no obligation to do so.[29]

Appellate review

In deciding whether a trial court has conducted an appropriate <u>Nelson</u> inquiry, appellate courts apply an abuse of discretion standard of review.[30] While a thorough and searching <u>Nelson</u> inquiry is always preferable when facially sufficient and timely allegations of ineffective assistance of counsel are made, an inadequate inquiry is subject to a harmless error analysis.[31] However, the appellate court should be careful not to ground its harmless error analysis on the quantum of evidence produced against the defendant at trial.[32] Rather, when reviewing an inadequate <u>Nelson</u> inquiry, an appellate court may still affirm the

---

[28] **Capehart v. State**, 583 So. 2d 1009 (Fla. 1991), *cert. denied*, 502 U.S. 1065 (1992).

[29] **State v. Craft**, 685 So. 2d 1292 (Fla. 1996).

[30] **Kearse v. State**, 605 So. 2d 534, 536 (Fla. 1st DCA 1992), *rev. denied*, 613 So. 2d 5 (Fla. 1993); **Moore v. State**, 778 So. 2d 1054 (Fla. 4th DCA 2001).

[31] **Kott v. State**, 518 So. 2d 957 (Fla. 1st DCA 1988); **Kinzie v. State**, 696 So. 2d 530 (Fla. 4th DCA 1997), *rev. denied*, 705 So. 2d 9 (Fla. 1997).

[32] **Graves v. State**, 642 So. 2d 142 (Fla. 4th DCA 1994).

conviction as long as there is no
evidence in the record of any
conflict or lack of communication
during the trial between the
defendant and court-appointed counsel
which would support a finding that
the defendant did not receive an
adequate defense.[33]

---

[33] **Kott**, 518 So. 2d at 958; **State v.
Marti**, 756 So. 2d 224 (Fla. 3d DCA 2000).

CHAPTER TWO

WHEN A DEFENDANT REQUESTS SELF-REPRESENTATION

The timing of the request

In 1975, the United States Supreme Court held in <u>Faretta v. California</u>, 422 U.S. 806 (1975) that a defendant in a state criminal trial has a constitutional right to proceed without counsel when he or she voluntarily and intelligently elects to do so. But the right to self-representation may be lost if it is not timely asserted. "<u>Faretta</u> does not deal with the situation of a defendant attempting to proceed pro se after trial has begun."[34] The point at which trial "begins", and therefore cuts off a defendant's unqualified right of self-representation, is fairly consistent

---

[34] **Bassette v. Thompson**, 915 F.2d 932 (4th Cir. 1990)(Trial court properly denied defendant's request to make his closing argument after proceeding through trial with counsel up to the time of closing), *cert. denied*, 499 U.S. 982 (1991); *see also* **Brown v. Wainright**, 665 F.2d 607 (11th Cir. 1982)(Request to assume defense prior to closing arguments on third day of trial held untimely); **Horton v. Dugger**, 895 F.2d 714 (11th Cir. 1990)(Upholding denial of self-representation request made after jury was empaneled but before trial began).

among the federal circuits.[35] In the Eleventh Circuit, which encompasses Florida, it has been held that a defendant's request to proceed pro se is untimely if it is not made before the jury is empaneled.[36]

It should be noted that at least one Florida court has held otherwise. In <u>Smith v. State</u>, 677 So. 2d 370 (Fla. 2d DCA 1996), the defendant sought to discharge his court-appointed counsel after the state had rested its case but before the defense case in chief. The trial court advised the defendant that he had "no choice" but to proceed with representation by counsel or return to his cell while the trial continued

---

[35] **Buhl v. Cooksey**, 233 F.3d 783, 795 (3d Cir. 2000)(Defendant's request for self-representation was timely because he first made it several weeks before trial and then reasserted the request the day before trial began); **United States v. Walker**, 142 F.3d 103, 109 (2d Cir. 1998)(Defendant's request for self-representation was untimely though made before empaneling the jury, because he asserted the request after 19 days of voir dire), *cert. denied*, 525 U.S. 896 (1998); **Savage v. Estelle**, 924 F.2d 1459, 1463 n. 7 (9th Cir. 1990)(Request for self-representation was timely because it was asserted before voir dire and thus before jury was empaneled), *cert. denied*, 501 U.S. 1255 (1991); **United States v. Lawrence**, 605 F.2d 1321, 1325 (4th Cir. 1979)(Request for self-representation was untimely because it was made after the jury had been selected but before it had been sworn).

[36] **United States v. Young**, 287 F.3d 1352 (11th Cir. 2002).

without him. In reversing the conviction, the Second District Court of Appeal held that the defendant did indeed have another choice available to him: self-representation. In light of the well-established federal case law on this issue, the Second District Court of Appeal may wish to revisit its holding in <u>Smith</u>.

The nature of the request

While the right to counsel is in force until it is waived, the right to self-representation does not attach until asserted.[37] A trial judge is only required to conduct a <u>Faretta</u> inquiry when there is an unequivocal request for self-representation.[38] By far the most frequently cited theory for why a defendant will elect to proceed pro se is that of trial strategy, as a means of invoking the jury's sympathy by projecting the image of a lone defendant against the mammoth state.[39] But a defendant is

---

[37] **Brown**.

[38] **Augsberger**; *see also* **Weems v. State**, 645 So. 2d 1098 (Fla. 4th DCA 1994), *rev. denied*, 654 So. 2d 920 (Fla. 1995).

[39] **Wiggins v. Estelle**, 681 F.2d 266, n. 16 (5th Cir. 1982), *rev'd on other grounds*, 465 U.S. 168 (1984). Another theory advanced by the **Wiggins** court is that a defendant may want the opportunity to be judged by the jury as a person, and hopefully decide all matters of credibility in his or her favor. A defendant adopting this strategy would

not required to give any justification at all for seeking self-representation.

Subsequent waiver of the right to self-representation

Even if a defendant makes a clear and unambiguous request to represent himself or herself, the right to self-representation may be waived through subsequent conduct indicating that he or she is vacillating on the issue or has abandoned the request altogether.[40] This is because the right of self-representation is waived more easily than the right to counsel, both before assertion of the right as well as after. For example, a defendant may be deemed to have waived the right to self-representation after he or she requests self-representation, but then allows appointed counsel to plea bargain on his or her behalf and accepts the terms of the bargain.[41] A waiver of the right to self-representation may occur by conduct alone, and without any inquiry into

---

view self-representation as a low-key approach to trial, conveying the impression that he or she has nothing to hide.

[40] **Brown**.

[41] **United States v. Montgomery**, 529 F.2d 1404 (10th Cir. 1976), *cert. denied*, 426 U.S. 908 (1976).

the knowing and voluntary nature of the relinquishment of the right.[42]

The nature of the *Faretta* inquiry

The purpose of a *Faretta* hearing is to determine whether a defendant is knowingly and intelligently waiving the right to counsel. While the Florida Supreme Court has approved a model colloquy for conducting a *Faretta* inquiry[43] which is included in the Appendix of this book, there are no particular words required to establish that the

---

[42] **Brown**.

[43] **In re Amendment to Florida Rule of Criminal Procedure 3.111(d)(2)-(3)**, 719 So. 2d 873 (Fla. 1998).

Just three years before the approval of this standardized colloquy, Judge Barfield expressed disdain at the prospect of the adoption of such a *pro forma* inquiry in his dissenting opinion in **Dortch v. State**, 651 So. 2d 154 (Fla. 1st DCA 1995), *overruled*, **Potts v. State**, 718 So. 2d 757 (Fla. 1998):

[O]ut there, somewhere, there is a litany that will satisfy appellate review. The trial judges need only find it. If they try very hard, it will happen. When it does, an appellate court will publish it. Then the trial judges can recite the same acceptable litany while each defendant affirmatively responds with all the intelligence of an amoeba, and it will be okay. I would script such a litany if I thought it were appropriate, but it is not. Artificially contriving a form to prevail over substance will not improve the quality of choice.

Dortch, 651 So. 2d at 158 (Barfield, J., dissenting).

defendant is making an informed
decision. The issue depends on the
facts and circumstances of each
case.[44] The ultimate test is not the
trial court's express advice, but
rather the defendant's
understanding.[45] So long as the record
as a whole establishes that a
defendant "knows what he is doing and
his choice is made with eyes open,"
the trial judge's decision to allow a
defendant to represent himself or
herself will be upheld.[46]

While the offer of assistance of
counsel must be renewed at all
subsequent critical stages as
explained later in this Chapter, the

---

[44] **Fitzpatrick v. Wainwright**, 800 F.2d
1057 (11th Cir. 1986); **Payne v. State**, 642
So. 2d 111 (Fla. 1st DCA 1994).

[45] **Fitzpatrick**.

[46] **Faretta**, 422 U.S. at 835; see also
United States v. McDowell, 814 F.2d 245 (6th
Cir. 1987)(Noting that, while a formal
deliberate and searching inquiry is
preferable, a nonformalistic approach of
reviewing the record as a whole may be used
to determine the sufficiency of the waiver),
cert. denied, 484 U.S. 980 (1987); **Baranko
v. State**, 406 So. 2d 1271 (Fla. 1st DCA
1981)(Although the court's formal inquiry
was minimal, the numerous pleadings filed by
the defendant reflected his familiarity with
the legal process, and he was articulate and
persuasive. "In light of these facts, we
cannot say that the court's inquiry, which
dealt primarily with the voluntariness of
appellant's decision, was insufficient."),
appeal after remand, 428 So. 2d 324 (Fla.
1st DCA 1983).

<u>Faretta</u> inquiry itself need not be repeated unless a different judge presides over subsequent critical stages, or the defendant gives the judge reason to believe that there has been "a diminution in [the defendant's] understanding of relevant matters [] since [the judge] conducted the <u>Faretta</u> hearing."[47]

Dangers and disadvantages of self-representation

Perhaps the most important aspect of the <u>Faretta</u> hearing is ensuring that the defendant is aware of the dangers and disadvantages of self-representation. Again, the nature of the advice a trial court is required to give depends on the facts and circumstances of each case and each defendant. In appropriate cases, courts have found some very brief discussions of the dangers and disadvantages of self-representation to meet the mandates of <u>Faretta</u>. For example, in <u>Potts v. State</u>, 698 So.

---

[47] **Nelson v. Alabama**, 15 Fla. L. Weekly Fed. C616 (11th Cir. June 3, 2002)(Same judge who conducted defendant's 1987 **Faretta** hearing was not required to conduct the hearing again before allowing the defendant to represent himself at his 1994 resentencing hearing; judge expressly stated that he was relying on the 1987 inquiry, and he observed no diminution in defendant's understanding of relevant matters in the years since the **Faretta** hearing was conducted).

2d 315 (Fla. 4th DCA 1997), *aff'd*, 718 So. 2d 757 (Fla. 1998), the appellate court held that the defendant was sufficiently advised of the dangers and disadvantages of self-representation when the judge twice advised the defendant that it would be a "big mistake" for him to represent himself, that she doubted he had sufficient legal knowledge to do an adequate job, and that he should let appointed counsel try the case. And in United States v. McDowell, 814 F.2d 245 (6th Cir. 1987), *cert. denied*, 484 U.S. 980 (1987), the trial judge's advice was held to be sufficient where he had repeatedly advised the defendant that he thought the defendant was making a mistake in representing himself and that he was "in over his head". A few Florida courts have even upheld convictions in cases where there was no advice at all about the dangers and disadvantages of self-representation, because the defendants had otherwise demonstrated an understanding of the court system.[48]

If the defendant is a practicing criminal attorney, he or she still has a Sixth Amendment right to

---

[48] **Baggett v. State**, 687 So. 2d 934 (Fla. 4th DCA 1997); **United States v. Hafen**, 726 F.2d 21 (1st Cir. 1984), *cited with approval in* **Butler v. State**, 767 So. 2d 534 (Fla. 4th DCA 2000).

independent counsel.[49] The trial court must still establish that the attorney-defendant has knowingly and intelligently waived the right to independent counsel before allowing him or her to engage in self-representation.[50] However, the defendant's status as an attorney may be considered by the court in determining whether a valid waiver has been made. Therefore while a complete *Faretta* inquiry is preferable with such defendants, it may not be required.[51]

Legal knowledge, skill and experience

By far the most complicated issue surrounding the requirement of a *Faretta* hearing is whether a trial judge should inquire into the defendant's legal skills and his or her ability to actually present a defense. In 1967, the Fourth District Court of Appeal in Cappetta v. State, 204 So. 2d 913 (Fla. 4th DCA 1967) established a test for determining whether "unusual circumstances" existed which would permit a trial judge to deny a defendant the right to self-representation:

In determining unusual circumstances, included but not limited thereto is whether

---

[49] **Butler**.
[50] **Id.**
[51] **Id.**

the accused, by reason of age, mental derangement, lack of knowledge, or education, or inexperience in criminal procedures *would be deprived of a fair trial if allowed to conduct his own defense,* or in any case, where the complexity of the crime was such that in the interest of justice legal representation was necessary.[52] [Emphasis added].

In reviewing the Fourth District's decision in <u>Cappetta</u>, the Florida Supreme Court reversed on other grounds but implicitly approved the "unusual circumstances" test.[53] Thereafter, the Fourth District instructed its trial courts to rely upon the <u>Cappetta</u> "unusual circumstances" test for guidance in deciding whether to discharge appointed counsel and allow a defendant to proceed pro se.[54]

In apparent accord with the "unusual circumstances" test, the 1972 version of Florida Rule of Criminal Procedure 3.111(d) read:

(3) No waiver shall be accepted if it appears that the defendant is unable to make an intelligent and understanding choice because of a mental condition, age,

---

[52] **Cappetta v. State**, 204 So. 2d 913, 918 (Fla. 4th DCA 1967).

[53] **State v. Cappetta**, 216 So. 2d 749 (Fla. 1968), *cert. denied*, 394 U.S. 1008 (1969); *see also* **Morris v. State**, 667 So. 2d 982, 986 (Fla. 4th DCA 1996), *app. dism.*, 673 So. 2d 29 (Fla. 1996).

[54] **Nelson v. State**.

education, experience, the nature or complexity of the case, or other factors.

When the United States Supreme Court subsequently rendered its six-to-three decision in <u>Faretta</u> in 1975, it held that a defendant's technical legal knowledge is irrelevant to an assessment of a knowing exercise of the right to conduct one's own defense. "The 'competent' language in <u>Faretta</u> is directed at the 'knowing and voluntary' nature of the defendant's choice, not at the ability of the defendant to mount a successful defense."[55] "Indeed, the Supreme Court's decision in <u>Godinez [v. Moran</u>, 509 U.S. 389 (1993)] explicitly forbids any attempt to measure a defendant's competency to waive the right to counsel by evaluating his ability to represent himself."[56]

Despite the fact that <u>Faretta</u> made <u>Cappetta</u>'s "unusual circumstances" test no longer viable, some Florida courts continued to allow the old test to infect post-<u>Faretta</u> case law.[57] The Second District Court of

---

[55] **Peters v. Gunn**, 33 F.3d 1190, 1192 (9th Cir. 1994).

[56] **United States v. Arlt**, 41 F.3d 516, 518 (9th Cir. 1994), *appeal after remand*, 85 F.3d 638 (9th Cir. 1996).

[57] *See e.g.*, **Robinson v. State**, 368 So. 2d 674 (Fla. 1st DCA 1979); **Smith v. State**, 407 So. 2d 894 (Fla. 1981); **Williams v. State**, 427 So. 2d 768 (Fla. 2d DCA 1983); **Smith v. State**, 444 So. 2d 542 (Fla. 1st DCA

Appeal eventually recognized the problem and receded from a long line of so-infected cases in <u>Bowen v. State</u>, 677 So. 2d 863 (Fla. 2d DCA 1996). The Second District's decision was approved by the Florida Supreme Court.[58] The supreme court's <u>Bowen</u> decision appears to be an implicit acknowledgment that Florida's pre-<u>Faretta</u> "unusual circumstances" test for self-representation established in <u>Cappetta</u> was overruled by <u>Faretta</u>.

In his concurring opinion in <u>Bowen</u>, Justice Wells suggested an immediate review of Florida Rule of Criminal Procedure 3.111(d), because he felt that it did not comport with post-<u>Faretta</u> law. It is easy to see why Justice Wells was concerned, as the version of the rule in effect at the time of the <u>Bowen</u> decision appeared at first glance to have been taken directly from the pre-<u>Faretta</u> "unusual circumstances" test established in <u>Cappetta</u>. Both the rule and the "unusual circumstances" test listed five factors that the trial judge should consider; indeed, four of them were virtually identical.

1984); **Ashcraft v. State**, 465 So. 2d 1374 (Fla. 2d DCA 1985); **Cerkella v. State**, 588 So. 2d 1058 (Fla. 3d DCA 1991).

[58] **Bowen v. State**, 677 So. 2d 863 (Fla. 2d DCA 1996), *aff'd*, 698 So. 2d 248 (Fla. 1997), *cert. denied*, 522 U.S. 1081 (1998).

Pursuant to Justice Wells' suggestion, Rule 3.111(d) was amended in 1998 to read:

(3) Regardless of the defendant's legal skills or the complexity of the case, the court shall not deny a defendant's unequivocal request to represent himself or herself, if the court makes a determination of record that the defendant has made a knowing and intelligent waiver of counsel.[59]

In light of <u>Bowen</u> and the new rule, trial judges may understandably be hesitant to make any inquiry at all into a defendant's knowledge of the law, legal skills, or experience in the criminal justice system. But such inquiry is not only permissible, it actually remains an integral part of the <u>Faretta</u> hearing. As the Second District stated in <u>Bowen</u>:

We emphasize, without reservation, that we do not intend to suggest that the trial court should not delve into those matters that have been labelled 'special circumstances.' In fact, <u>Faretta</u> *requires* that the defendant's age, education, mental status and experience with criminal proceedings be subjects of inquiry. Those factors, however, bear exclusively on *whether the defendant has made a knowing and intelligent waiver and not whether the defendant's responses would indicate exposure to an unfair trial.* [Emphasis in original].

---

[59] **In re Amendment to Florida Rule of Criminal Procedure**.

Prior to <u>Bowen</u>, the Fourth District had suggested that trial judges could inquire about the fairness of a trial without counsel when conducting a <u>Faretta</u> hearing, as long as the judge did not deny self-representation because of the defendant's lack of legal knowledge. According to the Fourth District, this fairness inquiry served the salutary purpose of making the defendant "aware of the disadvantages under which he is placing himself by waiving counsel."[60] But the supreme court's decision in <u>Bowen</u> now appears to prohibit any such fairness inquiry: "[O]nce a court determines that a competent defendant of his or her own free will has 'knowingly and intelligently' waived the right to counsel, the dictates of <u>Faretta</u> are satisfied, the inquiry is over, and the defendant may proceed unrepresented. [] The court may not inquire further into whether the defendant could provide himself with a substantively qualitative defense[.]"[61]

However <u>Bowen</u> should not be construed as imposing a blanket prohibition on a trial judge's consideration of the existence of "unusual circumstances" in deciding whether to allow self-representation. A trial judge may properly deny self-

---

[60] **Morris v. State**.

[61] **Bowen**, 698 So. 2d at 251.

representation on the ground that the defendant will not get a fair trial based on "unusual circumstances" such as the state of the defendant's health, as long as the "unusual circumstance" is something other than lack of legal knowledge.[62] But before such an "unusual circumstance" may be used to deny a defendant the right to self-representation, the trial court must conduct an evidentiary hearing to determine the potential impact on the right to a fair trial.[63]

While the new version of Rule 3.111(d)(3) comports with <u>Faretta</u> and the Florida Supreme Court's decision in <u>Bowen</u>, the amendment was actually unnecessary. There was one glaring distinction between the old version of Rule 3.111(d)(3) and <u>Cappetta</u>'s now-defunct "unusual circumstances" test. The "unusual circumstances" test provided that the five factors should be used to *determine whether a pro se defendant would be deprived of a fair trial* if allowed to conduct his or her own defense. Clearly this was in violation of <u>Faretta</u>, which held that whether a defendant receives a fair trial due to lack of legal skills is irrelevant. In contrast, the five very similar factors in the old Rule 3.111(d)(3)

---

[62] **Morris v. State**.

[63] **Kleinfeld v. State**, 568 So. 2d 937 (Fla. 4th DCA 1990), *rev. denied*, 581 So. 2d 167 (Fla. 1991), *appeal after remand*, 587 So. 2d 592 (Fla. 4th DCA 1991).

were specified to be used for the purpose of determining *whether the defendant's choice to proceed pro se was intelligent and understanding*, not whether they would result in the denial of a fair trial. In sum, even though the amendment to the rule was legally unnecessary, the extensive revision has eliminated any possibility of confusion due to the first-glance striking similarity between the old Rule 3.111(d)(3) and the now abandoned "unusual circumstances" test.

After the <u>Bowen</u> decision and the amendment to Rule 3.111(d)(3), the bottom line remains that nothing in <u>Faretta</u> or its progeny prohibits a judge from inquiring into a defendant's legal knowledge and skill, as long as that information is used exclusively to determine whether a defendant's waiver of counsel is knowing and intelligent.

Ability and willingness to abide by the rules of courtroom procedure and protocol

In <u>McKaskle v. Wiggins</u>, 465 U.S. 168 (1984), the United States Supreme Court held that a defendant must have the ability and willingness to abide by the rules of procedure and courtroom protocol before he or she may be permitted to engage in self-representation. The Ninth Circuit Court of Appeals has interpreted this requirement to mean that a trial court may deny self-representation to an accused whose severe speech impediment (which prevented him from communicating effectively with the jury) rendered him unable to abide by the rules of courtroom procedure.[64] The meaning of McKaskle has not been addressed to any great extent by Florida courts. To date the only interpretation of McKaskle in Florida has been to say that the case should not be understood to expand the elemental Faretta concept to include additional standards governing a trial court's implementation of the right to self-representation.[65] Florida courts should "merely interpret McKaskle as permitting denials of the Faretta right to an accused who is unable to abide by rules of courtroom procedure, just as the right may be denied to those who are unwilling to do so."[66]

If the trial judge concludes after a Faretta inquiry that the defendant's waiver is not knowing and intelligent, the judge should explain on the record the factors leading to the decision and then proceed to trial with the defendant represented by appointed counsel. On the other

---

[64] **Savage**, 924 F.2d at 1466.

[65] **Bowen v. State**, 677 So. 2d 863 (Fla. 2d DCA 1996).

[66] **Savage**, 924 F.2d at 1466, *cited in* **Bowen**, 677 So. 2d at 866.

hand, if the judge concludes that the defendant's waiver is knowing and intelligent, then the defendant must be permitted to represent himself or herself at trial.

Renewal of the offer of assistance of counsel

The trial judge should renew the offer of assistance of counsel at each subsequent stage of the proceedings.[67] The renewal of the offer of counsel should be made close enough in time to the commencement of trial to remind the defendant of the right he or she is relinquishing.[68] In Lamb v. State, 535 So. 2d 698 (Fla. 1st DCA 1988), the conviction was affirmed despite the fact that three weeks had passed between the pretrial hearing addressing the waiver of counsel and the commencement of trial, where the offer of counsel was not renewed on the morning of trial. In contrast, in Sproule v. State, 719 So. 2d 349 (Fla. 4th DCA 1998), the conviction was reversed when nearly a month had passed between the Faretta hearing and the commencement of

---

[67] **Fla. R. Crim. P. 3.111(d)(5) (2001).**

[68] See **Pall v. State**, 632 So. 2d 1084 (Fla. 2d DCA 1994)(Conviction reversed because there was a seven-month interval between waiver hearing and commencement of trial, and offer of assistance of counsel was not renewed on morning of trial).

trial, and the offer of counsel was not renewed on the morning of trial. The Sproule court specifically based its holding on the fact that the defendant had appeared at two more hearings between the Faretta hearing and the commencement of trial, and that neither of those intervening hearings re-addressed the issue of self-representation. Sproule and Lamb appear to indicate that if there are any intervening proceedings between the Faretta hearing and the commencement of trial, the offer of assistance of counsel must be renewed on the morning of trial, regardless of the time interval.

Once the offer of counsel has been renewed at trial, there is no need to renew the offer again until the commencement of post-trial proceedings such as sentencing. Specifically, there is no requirement to renew the offer of counsel at each stage *of trial*, i.e. before the presentation of the evidence or before closing arguments. This is because trial as a whole is one "stage of the proceedings".[69]

---

[69] **McCarthy v. State**, 731 So. 2d 778 (Fla. 4th DCA 1999); **Knight v. State**, 770 So. 2d 663 (Fla. 2000)("We deny relief on this claim because the trial court was not required to offer counsel during the same stage of the proceedings where Knight waived his right to counsel, the trial portion."), *cert. denied*, 532 U.S. 1011 (2001).

Unlike the review of an inadequate _Faretta_ inquiry and a record which fails to demonstrate the knowing and intelligent nature of the waiver of counsel, appellate courts are free to apply a harmless error analysis to the failure to renew the offer of counsel at a subsequent stage of the proceedings.[70]

Special Factors

Defendants who misbehave

The exercise of a defendant's right to self-representation "is not a license to abuse the dignity of the court or to frustrate orderly proceedings, and a defendant may not manipulate the proceedings by willy-nilly leaping back and forth between the choices."[71] A defendant who continues to vacillate between self-representation and representation by counsel may be required to proceed pro se through trial. But the mere fact that a defendant flip-flops between counsel and self-representation is insufficient, standing alone, for a judge to

---

[70] **Mincey v. State**, 684 So. 2d 236 (Fla. 1st DCA 1996); **Harris v. State**, 687 So. 2d 29 (Fla. 5th DCA 1997).

[71] **Jones v. State**, 449 So. 2d 253, 257 (Fla. 1984), _cert. denied_, 469 U.S. 893 (1984); _see also_ **State v. Roberts**, 677 So. 2d 264 (Fla. 1996).

conclude that a defendant is seeking to manipulate the trial process. Before a judge can force a defendant to proceed pro se in this situation, he or she should conduct an inquiry to elicit evidence and make express findings on the issue of bad faith manipulation.[72]

Occasionally a trial judge will be confronted with a defendant whose behavior and complaints regarding court-appointed counsel are completely unfounded and disruptive to courtroom procedure. In such a situation, the judge is not compelled to allow the defendant to delay and continually frustrate the trial. The judge may presume that the defendant's actions constitute a request to proceed pro se.[73] The best course would be to confirm the waiver of counsel by conducting a <u>Faretta</u> inquiry. But the failure to do so does not automatically require reversal. For example, in <u>Waterhouse v. State</u>, 596 So. 2d 1008 (Fla. 1992), *cert. denied*, 506 U.S. 957 (1992), the defendant's conviction was affirmed despite the lack of a <u>Faretta</u> hearing. "Waterhouse's manipulation of the proceedings and his attempts to delay show an obvious understanding of the proceedings against him. Under these facts, we

---

[72] **United States v. Proctor**, 166 F.3d 396 (1st Cir. 1999).

[73] **State v. Young**, 626 So. 2d 655 (Fla. 1993).

find the requirements of <u>Faretta</u> were met."[74]

Even if a defendant's misbehavior results in the forfeiture of counsel at trial, it does not necessarily follow that the defendant has forfeited the right to counsel at the next stage of the proceedings. The trial judge must still renew the offer of counsel prior to sentencing.[75]

Erroneous claims of insolvency

In order to demonstrate an entitlement to appointed counsel, the court must determine that the defendant meets the qualifications for indigency as articulated in §27.52, Fla. Stat. (2001). Sometimes a defendant will claim that he or she does not have the resources to hire private counsel and will ask the court to appoint an attorney even though he or she does not meet the statutory criteria for indigent status. In such a case, the court may properly deny appointed counsel to the defendant. However, the court must still conduct a <u>Faretta</u> inquiry before allowing the defendant to

---

[74] **Waterhouse v. State**, 596 So. 2d 1008, 1014-15 (Fla. 1992), *cert. denied*, 506 U.S. 957 (1992).

[75] **Watson v. State**, 718 So. 2d 253 (Fla. 2d DCA 1998), *appeal after remand*, 750 So. 2d 118 (Fla. 2d DCA 1999).

represent himself or herself at trial.[76] This is because "the language used in <u>Faretta</u> and [Florida Rule of Criminal Procedure 3.111(d)] draw[s] no distinction between solvent and insolvent defendants."[77]

Defendants who have mental problems

The competency to waive counsel and the competency to stand trial are the same, except for the fact that the waiver of the right to counsel must also be knowing and voluntary.[78] The single competency standard to be used in both situations is whether the defendant has "sufficient present ability to consult with his lawyer with a reasonable degree of rational understanding" and a "rational as well as factual understanding of the proceedings against him."[79] A higher standard is not necessary to ensure that a defendant is competent to represent himself or herself, because the ability to do so has no bearing upon the competency to choose self-representation.[80]

---

[76] **Morgano v. State**, 439 So. 2d 924 (Fla. 2d DCA 1983).

[77] **Miller v. State**, 485 So. 2d 1346 (Fla. 5th DCA 1986).

[78] **Godinez v. Moran**, 509 U.S. 389 (1993).

[79] **Dusky v. United States**, 362 U.S. 402 (1960).

[80] **Godinez**.

Juveniles

Faretta issues are somewhat different in the context of juvenile prosecutions. This is because "in the juvenile delinquency system rehabilitation is the principal focus, while in the adult criminal system punishment is the principal focus."[81]

A juvenile who has been accused of an offense punishable by incarceration in a juvenile corrections institution has a Sixth Amendment right to be represented by counsel.[82] As such, a juvenile must make a knowing and intelligent waiver of the right to counsel prior to being allowed to engage in self-representation.[83] The waiver inquiry for a juvenile "must be at least equal to that accorded an adult; nevertheless, [] a trial judge should be even more careful when accepting a waiver of counsel from a juvenile."[84] The "requirement of a detailed inquiry recognizes that '[i]t is extremely doubtful that any child of limited experience can possibly

---

[81] **State v. T.M.B.**, 716 So. 2d 269 (Fla. 1998).

[82] **Fla. R. Crim. P. 3.111(b)(1)**; **In re Gault**, 387 U.S. 1 (1967).

[83] **In Interest of D.C.T.**, 347 So. 2d 687 (Fla. 4th DCA 1977).

[84] **K.M. v. State**, 448 So. 2d 1124 (Fla. 2d DCA 1984).

comprehend the importance of counsel.'"[85]

Florida Rule of Juvenile Procedure 8.165(b) (2001) provides:

(3) No waiver shall be accepted where it appears that the party is unable to make an intelligent and understanding choice because of mental condition, age, education, experience, the nature or complexity of the case, or other factors.

Notably, this rule is almost identical to the old version of Florida Rule of Criminal Procedure 3.111(d)(3) which, based upon Justice Wells' suggestion in <u>Bowen v. State</u>, 698 So. 2d 248 (Fla. 1997), was completely overhauled in 1998. However as explained earlier in this Chapter, the old version of Rule 3.111(d)(3) was not constitutionally infirm, did not run afoul of <u>Faretta</u>, and therefore did not require amendment. Consequently the parallel Juvenile Rule 8.165(b), (which was not amended contemporaneously with Rule 3.111(d) and therefore remains viable), still comports with the requirements of <u>Faretta</u>. Even so, the Juvenile Court Rules Committee of the Florida Bar may wish to consider amending Juvenile Rule 8.165(b)(3) to mirror the new version of Criminal Rule 3.111(d)(3) in order to avoid confusion.

---

[85] **P.L.S. v. State**, 745 So. 2d 555, 557 (Fla. 4th DCA 1999)(quoting **G.L.D. v State**, 442 So. 2d 401, 404 (Fla. 2d DCA 1983)).

There is one additional requirement for obtaining a valid waiver of counsel from a juvenile rather than an adult. Florida Rule of Juvenile Procedure 8.165(a) (2001) places a duty upon the trial judge to obtain the child's waiver of counsel in writing if the waiver is made at the time of the entry of a plea or at the adjudicatory hearing. The rules provide a sample form for this purpose, which has been included in the Appendix.[86]

The issue of whether a juvenile's waiver of counsel is knowingly and intelligently made is fundamental and may be considered on appeal even though it was not presented to the trial court.[87] This holding applies regardless of whether the juvenile was convicted as a result of a trial or a plea.[88] The Florida Supreme Court has urged that Florida Rules of Criminal Procedure 3.800 and 3.850 be amended to apply to juveniles in order to avoid the necessity of the juvenile having to later challenge the voluntariness of a plea by petition for writ of habeas corpus.[89]

---

[86] **Fla. R. Juv. P. 8.933 (2001)**.

[87] **J.O. v. State**, 717 So. 2d 185 (Fla. 5th DCA 1998); **J.R.V. v. State**, 715 So. 2d 1135 (Fla. 5th DCA 1998).

[88] **State v. T.G.**, 800 So. 2d 204 (Fla. 2001).

[89] **Id.**

Self-representation in collateral proceedings

There is no Sixth Amendment right to counsel in state postconviction proceedings.[90] Since there is no constitutional right to collateral counsel, there can be no claim of ineffective assistance of collateral counsel.[91] It equally follows that no <u>Faretta</u> hearing is required before a defendant is permitted to represent himself or herself in a collateral proceeding.

The exception to this rule is that the Florida legislature has established a right to collateral counsel for death row inmates.[92] This right "was established to alleviate problems in obtaining counsel to represent Florida's death-sentenced prisoners in collateral relief proceedings[.]"[93] The legislature's creation of the Capital Collateral Representative in Chapter 27 Florida Statutes "did not add anything to the substantive state-law or constitu-

---

[90] **§924.066(3), Fla. Stat. (2001)**; **Pennsylvania v. Finley**, 481 U.S. 551 (1987); **Murray v. Giarratano**, 492 U.S. 1 (1989); **Lambrix v. State**, 698 So. 2d 247 (Fla. 1996), *cert. denied*, 522 U.S. 1122 (1998).

[91] **Lambrix**.

[92] **§27.7001, Fla. Stat. (2001)**.

[93] **Durocher v. Singletary**, 623 So. 2d 482, 483 (Fla. 1993).

tional rights of such persons."[94]
Therefore a death row inmate's
entitlement to collateral counsel is
a statutory right, not a
constitutional one. But since an
entitlement to counsel does exist,
the trial court must conduct a
"Faretta-type" inquiry before
allowing a death row inmate to
discharge counsel and proceed pro se
in a collateral proceeding.[95] The
focus of this inquiry should be on
the defendant's competency.[96] If the
"Faretta-type" hearing raises
questions in the judge's mind about
the defendant's competency, he or she
may order a mental health evaluation
and thereafter make a competency
determination.[97]

---

[94] **Id.**

[95] **Durocher**; **Sanchez-Velasco v. State**,
702 So. 2d 224 (Fla. 1997), *cert. denied*,
525 U.S. 811 (1998).

[96] **Durocher**.

[97] **Id.**

CHAPTER THREE

STANDBY COUNSEL AND HYBRID REPRESENTATION

Often a defendant seeking self-representation will request that standby counsel be appointed to assist the defendant in conducting his or her defense. The appointment of standby counsel under _Faretta_ is constitutionally permissible, but not constitutionally required. As a practical matter, standby counsel is usually denied only when the defendant refuses to cooperate with the trial court or previously-appointed counsel in their efforts to provide legal assistance.[98] However, in the future the Florida Legislature may wish to consider amending Chapter 27 Florida Statutes to explicitly prohibit the appointment of publicly-funded standby counsel for indigents who choose to be self-represented, unless the court elects to appoint standby counsel for its own convenience.

Only duly licensed members of the bar should be permitted to act as standby counsel. The trial judge is not required to allow a non-lawyer to

---

[98] **Jones v. State**, 449 So. 2d 253 (Fla. 1984), _cert. denied_, 469 U.S. 893 (1984).

assist a pro se defendant in lieu of a licensed attorney.[99]

Even if standby counsel is appointed, the defendant must be permitted to control the organization and content of his or her defense, make motions, argue points of law, participate in voir dire, question witnesses, and address the court and the jury at appropriate points. The defendant has the entire responsibility for his or her own defense.[100] The defendant does not have the right to require standby counsel to perform every function the defendant sees fit, whenever he or she sees fit.[101]

Sometimes a defendant will resist the appointment of standby counsel even though the trial judge believes an attorney's assistance might at some point become necessary. "A defendant does not have a constitutional right to receive personal instruction from the trial judge on courtroom procedure. Nor does the Constitution require judges to take over chores for a pro se defendant that would normally be attended to by trained counsel as a

---

[99] **Bauer v. State**, 610 So. 2d 1326 (Fla. 2d DCA 1992).

[100] **McKaskle**; **Behr v. Bell**, 665 So. 2d 1055 (Fla. 1996).

[101] **Aycock v. State**, 769 So. 2d 523 (Fla. 5th DCA 2000), *app. dism.*, 786 So. 2d 1183 (Fla. 2001).

matter of course."[102] In light of this, a trial judge can appoint standby counsel over the defendant's objection to relieve the judge of the need to explain and enforce basic rules of courtroom procedure or to assist the defendant in overcoming routine obstacles to reach his or her goal. However, the judge must not permit standby counsel's participation over the defendant's objection to substantially interfere with any significant tactical decisions, or to control the questioning of witnesses, or to speak on any matter of importance. Outside the presence of the jury, the defendant must be freely permitted to address the court on his or her own behalf. On disagreements between counsel and the defendant, the trial judge must resolve the conflict in the defendant's favor whenever the matter is one that would normally be left to the discretion of counsel.[103]

Occasionally a defendant will insist on acting as co-counsel with his court-appointed attorney. But Faretta does not require a trial judge to permit this type of hybrid representation. A defendant does not have the right to partially represent himself or herself and at the same time be partially represented by

---

[102] McKaskle.
[103] Id.

counsel.[104] Nonetheless, it is within the trial judge's discretion to allow a defendant to act as co-counsel with the attorney.[105] A trial judge should use extreme caution in allowing such an arrangement. This form of hybrid representation is generally disfavored, as it is "[o]ne of the most difficult and confusing components of the right to self-representation[.]"[106]

If a trial judge elects to allow a defendant to proceed as co-counsel at trial, it is unclear whether a Faretta inquiry is required. In Cason v. State, 652 So. 2d 1191 (Fla. 3d DCA 1995), the Third District noted that "the defendant never made an unequivocal request to do other than act as co-counsel with his court-appointed attorney. Consequently, a Faretta hearing was never triggered[.]" In Bell v. State, 699 So. 2d 674 (Fla. 1997), *cert. denied*, 522 U.S. 1123 (1998), the supreme court stated that because the defendant never "request[ed] to act alone as his own counsel," the trial

---

[104] **Id.**

[105] *See e.g.*, **United States v. Kimmel**, 672 F.2d 720 (9th Cir. 1982).

[106] John F. Decker, **The Sixth Amendment Right to Shoot Oneself in the Foot: An Assessment of the Guarantee of Self-Representation Twenty Years After Faretta**, 6 Seton Hall Const. L.J. 483, 537-540 (1996), *cited in* **Brooks v. State**, 703 So. 2d 504 (Fla. 1st DCA 1997).

court was not required to comply with _Faretta_. The following year in reliance upon _Bell_, the Second District held that a full _Faretta_ hearing was unnecessary because the defendant "was very clear that he wanted to assist his attorney."[107]

In contrast, the First District has held in Brooks v. State, 703 So. 2d 504 (Fla. 1st DCA 1997) that a trial court errs in failing to conduct a _Faretta_ inquiry when a defendant acts as co-counsel and undertakes any portion of his or her defense. The First District found that the defendant in _Brooks_ had conducted a "core function" of a lawyer by filing a few pretrial motions and giving the opening statement.

The eventual harmonization of the case law on this issue may well result in a rule that a _Faretta_ inquiry is required when a defendant acts as co-counsel only if the defendant's participation constitutes a "core function" of a lawyer. In order for trial judges to avoid having to delve into the exact nature of a defendant's participation and whether that participation constitutes a "core function" of a lawyer, the better practice would be to conduct a _Faretta_ inquiry any time a defendant is permitted to act as

---

[107] **Baker v. State**, 745 So. 2d 1035 (Fla. 2d DCA 1999).

co-counsel, regardless of the extent
of his or her participation.

CHAPTER FOUR

THE APPEAL PROCESS

Self-representation on appeal

The status of an accused changes dramatically when a jury returns a guilty verdict. The right to appeal after a criminal conviction is not grounded in the Constitution but is instead purely a creature of statute.[108] Even so, every state including Florida has chosen to allow such review. If a state has provided for appellate review, its appellate procedures must comport with the demands of due process and equal protection.[109]

The United States Supreme Court has held that "neither the holding nor the reasoning in Faretta requires [a state] to recognize a constitutional right to self-representation on direct appeal from a criminal conviction."[110] This is because trial is essentially a fact finding process, while the prosecution of an appeal requires the

---

[108] **Abney v. United States**, 431 U.S. 651 (1977).

[109] **Evitts v. Lucey**, 469 U.S. 387, 393 (1985).

[110] **Martinez v. California**, 528 U.S. 152 (2000).

raising of legal issues. Therefore
the personal input of the defendant
is far less significant at the
appellate level than at trial.[111]
Perhaps more importantly, the right
to counsel on appeal stems from the
Due Process and Equal Protection
Clauses of the Fourteenth Amendment,
(not from the Sixth Amendment, which
is the foundation on which <u>Faretta</u> is
based),[112] and the denial of self-
representation at the appellate level
does not violate due process or equal
protection guarantees.[113]

Of course, appellate courts may
still exercise their discretion and
allow a defendant to proceed pro se
with briefing and/or oral argument.[114]
Florida courts have indicated that
the exercise of this discretion may
be appropriate in cases where a
defendant has demonstrated legal
knowledge and skill, such as when he
or she is a trained paralegal.[115]

There is one exception to the
general rule that a defendant does
not have a right to self-
representation on appeal. The United
States Supreme Court has established
what has become known as the "<u>Anders</u>

---

[111] **Grant v. State**, 780 So. 2d 131 (Fla.
4th DCA 2000).

[112] *See* **People v. Scott**, 75 Cal. Rptr. 2d
315 (Cal. Ct. App. 1998).

[113] **Id.**

[114] **Martinez**.

[115] **Grant**.

procedure" for cases in which appointed counsel has examined the appellate record and is unable to make a good-faith argument that any error occurred at the trial level.[116] In such a case, counsel should so advise the appellate court and request permission to withdraw. The request must be accompanied by a brief referring to anything in the record that might arguably support the appeal, and a copy of counsel's brief must be furnished to the indigent defendant.[117] Then the defendant must be permitted to file a pro se brief to raise any points he or she chooses.[118] After giving the defendant the opportunity to submit a pro se brief, the appellate court must undertake a full and independent examination of the record to decide whether the appeal is wholly frivolous.[119] If the court finds that any legal points are arguable on the merits, prior to making a decision the defendant must be afforded the assistance of counsel to argue the

---

[116] **Anders v. California**, 386 U.S. 738 (1967).

[117] **Id.**

[118] **Id.**; **In re Anders Briefs**, 581 So. 2d 149 (Fla. 1991).

[119] **Anders v. California**; **State v. Davis**, 290 So. 2d 30 (Fla. 1974); **In re Anders Briefs**. The appellate court is required to conduct its full and independent review of the record even if the defendant elects not to file a pro se brief. **Id.**

appeal.[120]   But   these   special
considerations   do   not   entitle
defendants pursuing Anders appeals to
any priority or expedited review over
earlier-matured   cases   in   the
appellate court.[121]

In Coupe v. State, 564 So. 2d 1199
(Fla. 1st DCA 1990), the First
District Court of Appeal addressed
the question of what, if any, issues
may be raised by counsel in an
initial appellate brief without
losing the defendant's right to the
Anders procedure. The First District
concluded that it would "accept
briefs in accordance with Anders
which find no error as to the trial
or plea proceedings, but which
identify sentencing errors, except
where it is argued that the trial
court's reasons for departing from
the sentencing guidelines were
legally insufficient."[122] The Florida
Supreme Court approved Coupe with one
modification. The supreme court did
not agree with the First District's
conclusion   that   the   only
"sufficiently substantive" type of
sentencing issue which would preclude
the Anders procedure is an allegation
that the trial court relied on

---

[120] **Anders v. California**; **In re Anders Briefs**.

[121] **Hudson v. State**, 767 So. 2d 664 (Fla. 1st DCA 2000), *rev. denied*, 786 So. 2d 580 (Fla. 2001).

[122] **Coupe v. State**, 564 So. 2d 1199, 1200-01 (Fla. 1st DCA 1990).

insufficient grounds to depart from the guidelines. The court stated that there may be other sentencing errors which are sufficiently substantive in nature to warrant adversarial presentation to an appellate court with the assistance of counsel.[123] The raising of these "sufficiently substantive" sentencing issues by appellate counsel would bar the defendant from availing himself or herself of the <u>Anders</u> procedure. The defendant would lose the right to file a pro se brief, and he or she would not be entitled to a full and independent review of the record by the appellate court.

Appellate review of <u>Nelson</u>/<u>Faretta</u> issues

Because the trial court's decision regarding whether a defendant has made a knowing and intelligent waiver of the right to counsel turns primarily on an assessment of demeanor and credibility, its decision is entitled to great weight. The decision will be affirmed on review by an appellate court if it is supported by competent and substantial evidence in the record.[124]

The Florida Supreme Court has held that a harmless error analysis is

---

[123] **In re Anders Briefs**.

[124] **Potts v. State**, 718 So. 2d 757, 759 (Fla. 1998).

inapplicable to criminal cases in which the trial judge fails to conduct a sufficient <u>Faretta</u> inquiry.[125] But the supreme court has also held that "while a waiver hearing expressly addressing the disadvantages of a pro se defense is much to be preferred, it is not absolutely necessary."[126] The harmonization of these two rules of law leads to the conclusion that appellate courts are precluded from engaging in a harmless error analysis of an insufficient <u>Faretta</u> inquiry only when the record as a whole does not otherwise reflect that the waiver of counsel was knowing and intelligent.[127] The supreme court's statement in <u>Potts</u> that competent and substantial evidence "in the record" is required to uphold the trial

---

[125] **State v. Young**, 626 So. 2d 655 (Fla. 1993).

[126] **Rogers v. Singletary**, 698 So. 2d 1178 (Fla. 1996).

[127] *See* **Fitzpatrick** ("If the trial record demonstrates that Fitzpatrick's decision to represent himself was made with an understanding of the risks of self-representation, the knowing, intelligent, and voluntary waiver standard of the Sixth Amendment will be satisfied. So long as the record establishes that Fitzpatrick "[knew] what he [was] doing and his choice [was] made with eyes open," the trial judge's decision to allow Fitzpatrick to represent himself will be upheld."); *see also* footnote 46 in Chapter Two.

court's ruling supports this interpretation.

Several other cases also lend support to this view. In <u>Mundy v. State</u>, 687 So. 2d 1314 (Fla. 1st DCA 1996), *rev. denied*, 697 So. 2d 1217 (Fla. 1997), the First District applied a harmless error analysis to the court's failure to advise the defendant that if appointed counsel was discharged, the state would not be required to provide alternative representation. The court engaged in the harmless error analysis despite noting that "[i]t is not entirely clear whether a harmless error analysis is applicable in these circumstances." The court found that the error was not harmless because "there is nothing in the record to suggest that appellant was aware of that right."

More recently, in <u>Butler v. State</u>, 767 So. 2d 534 (Fla. 4th DCA 2000), the Fourth District affirmed a conviction in which the defendant represented himself but no <u>Faretta</u> hearing was conducted. While avoiding any overt discussion of the applicability of a harmless error analysis, <u>Butler</u> cited with approval a New Jersey case which held that the trial court's failure to advise the defendant of the dangers of self-representation was harmless where the record established that the defendant had a bachelor's degree in business law, had previously represented himself successfully in a criminal trial, and had several felony convictions.[128] <u>Butler</u> also quoted extensively from a federal case which held, "the totality of the evidence shows that [the defendant] knowingly and intelligently waived his right to counsel."[129]

In sum, if there was an inadequate <u>Faretta</u> inquiry at trial, the conviction may still be affirmed if the record otherwise reflects that the defendant's waiver of counsel was knowing and intelligent. But if there was an inadequate <u>Faretta</u> hearing and the record as a whole fails to reflect a knowing and intelligent waiver of counsel, an appellate court is precluded from holding such omissions harmless based on a finding that the defendant received a fair trial. As explained in Chapter Two, pursuant to the Florida Supreme Court's decision in <u>Bowen</u>, whether the defendant had sufficient legal knowledge and skill to enable him or her to receive a fair trial is irrelevant.

---

[128] **State v. Cirsafi**, 608 A.2d 317, 322-25 (N.J. 1992).

[129] **United States v. Campbell**, 874 F.2d 838 (1st Cir. 1989).

CONCLUSION

Very often a defendant's dissatisfaction with counsel stems from a lack of understanding that it is the attorney, not the defendant, who is ultimately in charge of strategic decisions. An attorney may choose to forego certain avenues of defense, and that decision is often difficult for a defendant who may have limited education and legal experience to accept. The best attorney-client working relationships are those in which the defendant is able to *mentally* relinquish control over the strategic decisions related to his or her case - control to which the defendant was never *legally* entitled in the first place.[130] When it comes right down to it, it is a

---

[130] The accused retains the ultimate authority to make certain fundamental decisions regarding his or her case, such as whether to plead guilty, waive a jury, testify in his or her own behalf, or take an appeal. *See* **Jones v. Barnes**, 463 U.S. 745 (1983). Several federal circuit courts have construed this list to be exhaustive. *See* **Sistrunk v. Vaughn**, 96 F.3d 666, 670 (3rd Cir. 1996); **United States v. Boyd**, 86 F.3d 719, 723 (7th Cir. 1996), *cert. denied*, 520 U.S. 1231 (1997). The Eleventh Circuit Court of Appeals, whose jurisdiction encompasses Florida, has to date declined to decide whether the **Jones** list is exhaustive. But the Eleventh Circuit is clearly reluctant to expand it. *See* **United States v. Burke**, 257 F.3d 1321 (11th Cir. 2001).

decision to trust one's attorney, to support and augment his or her efforts, which forges the best chance of success in the courtroom. As more than one appellate court has acknowledged, Florida's Offices of the Public Defender provide exemplary representation for indigent defendants.[131] The overwhelming majority of complaints of ineffective assistance of counsel are unwarranted.

---

[131] *See* **Young v. State**, 718 So. 2d 203 (Fla. 4th DCA 1998)("The Public Defender of the Fifteenth Judicial Circuit is exemplary in the representation that it provides to its clients both in the quality of the work and its efficiency."), *appeal after remand,* 739 So. 2d 1179 (Fla. 4th DCA 1999); **Floyd v. Parole and Probation Commission**, 509 So. 2d 919 (Fla. 1987)("We wish to recognize the excellent services rendered by Michael E. Allen, Public Defender of the Second Judicial Circuit, who this Court appointed to represent petitioner in this proceeding."); **Sanders v. State**, 450 So. 2d 907 (Fla. 4th DCA 1984)(Complimenting the offices of the Public Defender for the Fifteenth and Nineteenth Circuits. "We are confident that these offices are fulfilling their statutory responsibilities[.]"); **Shaw v. State**, 756 So. 2d 1101 (Fla. 4th DCA 2000)(Commending the "excellent brief" written by the public defender); **Dagostino v. State**, 675 So. 2d 194 (Fla. 4th DCA 1996)("[W]e have a very high regard for the Public Defender's office in this District and the quality of the representation which they furnish to the indigent appellants they serve."), *rev. denied,* 683 So. 2d 482 (Fla. 1996).

But despite best efforts of all parties, sometimes a defendant simply cannot or will not accept the assistance of court-appointed counsel. In such a case, a defendant has the comfort of knowing that self-representation is an option. As the United States Supreme Court observed in Faretta, "[w]hat were contrived as protections for the accused should not be turned into fetters … [T]o deny him in the exercise of his free choice the right to dispense with some of these safeguards [] is to imprison a man in his privileges and call it the Constitution."[132]

---

[132] **Faretta**, 422 U.S. at 815.

APPENDIX

TRIAL STAGE **FARETTA** INQUIRY

Right to Counsel Section:

1. Do you understand that you have a right to a lawyer? If you cannot afford to hire your own lawyer, and if you qualify for a court-appointed lawyer, one will be appointed for you.
2. The State of Florida will pay for a lawyer to advise you in these proceedings.
3. Shall I appoint a lawyer to represent you in this case?

[Continue to the next section only if the defendant says he or she does NOT want a lawyer].

Advantages Section:

4. I would like to explain to you some of the ways that having a lawyer to represent you can be to your advantage:

A. _Pre-trial_: *[Read only if applicable to current posture of case].*
A lawyer's legal knowledge and experience may favorably affect bail or pretrial release possibilities; may result in obtaining information about the case through skillful use of discovery devices; may uncover potential violations of

constitutional rights and take effective measures to address them; may ensure compliance with speedy trial and statute of limitations provisions; and may identify and secure favorable evidence to be introduced later at trial on your behalf.

B. *At trial*:

- A lawyer has the experience and knowledge of the entire process. [He/she] will argue for your side during the whole trial and present the best legal argument for your defense.
- Since jury qualification and selection are governed by numerous legal procedures, a lawyer's knowledge and experience may enhance the selection process on your behalf.
- A lawyer can call witnesses for you, question witnesses against you, and present evidence on your behalf.
- A lawyer can advise you on whether you should testify, the consequences of that decision, and what you have a right not to say.
- A lawyer has studied the rules of evidence and knows what evidence can or cannot come into your trial.
- A lawyer may provide assistance in ensuring that the jury is given complete and accurate jury instructions by the court, may

make effective closing arguments on your behalf, and may prevent improper argument by the prosecutor.
- A lawyer may ensure that any errors committed during trial are properly preserved for appellate review later by a higher court.

C. *Post-trial*:

- If you are convicted, a lawyer's assistance may be useful in preparing for sentencing, ensuring that favorable facts are brought to the attention of the court; ensuring that the court is advised of all legally available favorable dispositions; and in ensuring that the sentence is lawfully imposed.
- An attorney's legal knowledge and experience may be useful in filing an appeal and in seeking release on bail pending the appeal.

Dangers and Disadvantages Section:

5. As it is almost always unwise to represent yourself in court, let me tell you a few of the disadvantages of representing yourself:

- Do you understand that you will not get any special treatment from the court just because you are representing yourself?
- Do you understand that you will not be entitled to a continuance

simply because you want to represent yourself?

- *[Read if defendant is in custody]*: You will also be limited to the legal resources that are available to you while you are in custody. You will not be entitled to any additional library privileges just because you are representing yourself. A lawyer has fewer restrictions in researching your defense. Do you understand that?
- You are not required to possess the legal knowledge or skills of an attorney in order to represent yourself. However, you will be required to abide by the rules of criminal law and the rules of courtroom procedure. These laws took lawyers years to learn and abide by. If you demonstrate an unwillingness to abide by these rules, I may terminate your self-representation. Do you understand that?
- Do you understand that if you are disruptive in the courtroom that the court can terminate your self-representation and remove you from the courtroom, in which case the trial would continue without your presence?
- Do you understand that your access to the State Attorney who is prosecuting you will be severely reduced as compared to a lawyer who could easily contact the State Attorney?

- In addition, the State will not go easier on you or give you any special treatment because you are representing yourself. The State will present its case against you as an experienced lawyer.
- [*Read only if a stay-away order is in effect*]: Because a "stay-away" order is in effect against you, you will be prohibited from contacting the victim or any other witnesses who are a part of the "stay away" order. But if you are represented by an attorney, your attorney is allowed to speak to these people and question them regarding their testimony.
- And finally, if you are convicted, you cannot claim on appeal that your own lack of legal knowledge or skill constitutes a basis for a new trial. In other words, you cannot claim that you received ineffective assistance of counsel.

Do you understand these dangers and disadvantages of representing yourself?

Do you have any questions about these dangers and disadvantages?

Charges and Consequences Section:

6. Have you received and read a copy of the charges against you?
7. Do you understand all the charges against you?
8. During the time that you were represented by counsel in this

case, did you discuss this case with [him/her]?

9. Let me advise you of the possible penalties if you are found guilty of all the charges.

10. [*Read only if applicable*]: Do you understand that if you are convicted you may receive an enhanced sentence because:

- [*the State is seeking to sentence you as an [**habitual offender**]*
- [*it is alleged that you used a* **firearm** *in the commission of the offense*]
- [*it is alleged you wore a* **mask** *during the commission of the offense*]?

11. If you are found guilty by the [jury/court], the maximum [jail/prison] sentence you could receive is ____, and the minimum [jail/prison] sentence is ____.

12. You may be required to report to a probation or community control officer for [*length of time*].

13. You may be required to pay a fine or restitution.

14. You may have a permanent criminal record.

15. Do you understand that if you are not a citizen of the United States, and if you are found guilty you could be deported from this country, excluded from entering this country in the future, and denied the

opportunity to become a naturalized citizen?

16. Do you have any questions about the charges or the possible consequences and penalties if you are found guilty as I have explained them to you?

Competency to Waive Counsel Section:

17. I need to ask you a few questions about yourself to determine if you are competent to make a knowing and intelligent waiver of counsel.

- How old are you?
- Can you read? Can you write? Do you have any difficulty understanding English?
- How many years of school have you completed?
- Are you currently under the influence of any drugs or alcohol?
- Have you ever been diagnosed and treated for a mental illness?
- Do you have any physical problem which would hinder your self-representation in this case, such as a hearing problem, speech impediment, or poor eyesight?
- Has anyone told you not to use a lawyer?
- Has anyone threatened you if you hire a lawyer or accept a lawyer appointed by the court?
- Do you understand that a lawyer appointed by the court will represent you for free?

- Have you ever represented yourself in a trial? What was the outcome of that case?
- Do you have any questions about having a lawyer appointed to defend you?

18. Having been advised of your right to counsel, the advantages of having counsel, the disadvantages and dangers of proceeding without counsel, the nature of the charges and the possible consequences in the event of a conviction, are you certain that you do not want me to appoint a lawyer to defend you?

[Read only if defendant still does NOT want counsel and court desires defendant to have standby counsel]:

19. If I allow you to represent yourself and if you request it, I could have the Assistant Public Defender act as standby counsel. [He/she] would be available to you if you have any questions in the course of these proceedings. Would you like standby counsel?

   [Read if the defendant answers YES]:

20. I will appoint standby counsel to assist you. However, you will still be responsible for the organization and content of presenting your case. You still

have the entire responsibility for your own defense. Do you understand that?

[*Make findings on the record as to whether defendant is competent to waive counsel, and whether his/her waiver of counsel is knowing and intelligent*].

[*Renew offer of counsel at each subsequent stage of the proceeding*].

PLEA STAGE <u>FARETTA</u> INQUIRY

Right to Counsel Section:

1. Do you understand that you have a right to a lawyer?

- The State of Florida and the United States Constitution guarantee you the right to a lawyer.
- If you cannot afford to hire your own lawyer, and if you qualify for a court-appointed lawyer, I will appoint a lawyer for you right now.
- The State of Florida will even pay for this lawyer to help you with this decision as to whether or not to enter a plea.

2. Shall I appoint a lawyer to represent you?

[*Continue to the next section only if the defendant says he or she does NOT want a lawyer*].

Dangers and Disadvantages Section:

3. Let me tell you a few ways a lawyer might help you:

- A lawyer can advise you as to whether entering a plea is in your best interest.

- A lawyer has the experience to help you work with the State and even bargain for different terms.
- A lawyer can tell you the advantages and disadvantages of what you might say to the court during your plea hearing and the sentencing hearing that will follow.
- Do you understand that you will not get any special consideration from the court just because you are representing yourself?

4. Do you understand how necessary a lawyer is and how [he/she] could help you?

Consequences of the Plea Section:

5. You are currently charged with [*state offenses and their degrees*].

- Have you received a copy of these charges and had a chance to review them?
- Do you understand the serious nature of the charges against you?

6. If you decide to enter a plea, you will [*go over terms of plea*].

- The maximum sentence that can be imposed against you is ____.
- You may be forced to report to a probation or community control officer for [*length of time*].

- You may be required to pay a fine or restitution.
- You may have a permanent criminal record.
- If you are not a citizen of the United States, you could be deported from this country, excluded from entering this country in the future, and be denied the opportunity to become a naturalized citizen.
- Do you understand these consequences of entering a plea?
- Do you have any questions about these consequences?

7. If you do not fulfill the conditions of your plea, the State can ask to revoke your probation or community control and you could be arrested and brought back to court for a revocation hearing.
8. Do you understand the consequences of any violation of probation or community control?

Competency to Waive Counsel Section:

9. I need to ask you a few questions about yourself to determine if you are competent to make a knowing and intelligent waiver of counsel.

- How old are you?
- Can you read? Can you write? Do you have any difficulty understanding English?

- How many years of school have you completed?
- Are you currently under the influence of any drugs or alcohol?
- Have you ever been diagnosed and treated for a mental illness?
- Has anyone told you not to use a lawyer?
- Has anyone threatened you if you either hire a lawyer or accept one appointed by the court?
- Do you understand that a lawyer appointed by the court will represent you for free?
- Do you have any questions about having a lawyer appointed to defend you?

10. Having been advised of your right to an attorney, the advantages of having an attorney, the disadvantages of proceeding without an attorney, the nature of the charges against you, and the consequences of entering a plea, are you sure you do not want me to appoint a lawyer to represent you at this plea hearing?

[*Continue only if defendant insists he/she does NOT want an attorney and court desires defendant to have standby counsel*].

11. If I allow you to represent yourself and if you request it, I could have the Assistant Public Defender act as standby counsel.

He or she would be available to you if you have any questions in the course of these proceedings.

- Would you like me to appoint standby counsel to assist you?

[*Read only if defendant ACCEPTS standby counsel*]:

12. I will appoint standby counsel to assist you. However, you will still bear the entire responsibility for your case at the plea hearing. Do you understand that?

[*Make findings on the record as to whether defendant is competent to waive counsel, and whether his/her waiver of counsel is knowing and intelligent*].

[*After taking the plea, renew offer of counsel prior to imposing sentence*].

FORM 8.933 JUVENILE WAIVER OF COUNSEL

I, the undersigned child, _____ years of age, understand:

(1) That a complaint of delinquency alleging that I did _____ has been made against me;

(2) That I have a right to a lawyer and that if I am unable to pay a lawyer and wish to have one appointed, a lawyer will be provided immediately.

I understand this right to and offer of a lawyer and, being aware of the effect of this waiver, I knowingly, intelligently, understandingly and of my own free will now choose to and, by the signing of this waiver, do hereby waive my right to a lawyer and elect to proceed in this case without benefit of a lawyer.

DATE: _____ _____
CHILD

This waiver of counsel was signed in the presence of the undersigned witnesses who, by their signature, attest to its voluntary execution by this child.

WITNESS: _____
WITNESS: _____

Page 1 of 2

STATEMENT OF PARENT OR
RESPONSIBLE ADULT

This waiver of counsel was read by me and explained fully to this child in my presence. I understand the right of this child to an attorney and as the _____ of this child I consent to a waiver of this right.

Date: _____

_____

ORDER ASSESSING ATTORNEY'S FEE

The child herein, having been represented by the Public Defender in this cause pursuant to Section 27.52, Florida Statutes, it is

ORDERED AND ADJUDGED that a reasonable attorney's fee for services rendered by the Public Defender to the child in this cause is $_____ and that said fee is hereby assessed against _____, the father and _____, the mother, in favor of the State of Florida.

DONE AND ORDERED at _____, Florida, on _____ (date)_____.

_____
Circuit Judge

About The Author

Angela D. McCravy graduated magna cum laude with a B.S. degree in criminal justice from Georgia State University in 1983. Ten years later she graduated with honors from Stetson University College of Law in Gulfport, Florida with a juris doctor degree.

Formerly a staff attorney for the criminal division judges in Florida's Sixth Judicial Circuit, Ms. McCravy currently lives in Daytona Beach, Florida, where she is an Assistant Attorney General in the criminal law division of Florida's Office of the Attorney General. She practices regularly in the Fifth District Court of Appeal and the Florida Supreme Court, and has also been admitted to practice in the Middle District of Florida, the Eleventh Circuit Court of Appeals, and the United States Supreme Court.

Ms. McCravy has previously published articles and lectured on <u>Faretta</u> and <u>Nelson</u> issues. This is her first book.

NOTES

NOTES

NOTES

NOTES

NOTES

NOTES

NOTES

NOTES

NOTES

NOTES

NOTES

NOTES

NOTES

NOTES